MY FIRST BOOK

ENGLAND

ALL ABOUT ENGLAND FOR KIDS

GL🌐BED

CHILDREN BOOKS

Interior and cover Design: Daniel Day
Editor: Margaret Bam

For My Sons, Daniel, David and Jude

City view of London

England

England is a **country**.

A country is land that is controlled by a **single government**. Countries are also called **nations, states, or nation-states**.

Countries can be **different sizes**. Some countries are big and others are small.

The Cotswolds, England

Where Is England?

England is located in the continent of **Europe.**

A continent is **a massive area of land that is separated from others by water or other natural features**.

England is situated in the western part of Europe.

Oxford Street, London

Capital

The capital of England is London

London is located in the **southern part** of the country.

London is the largest city in England.

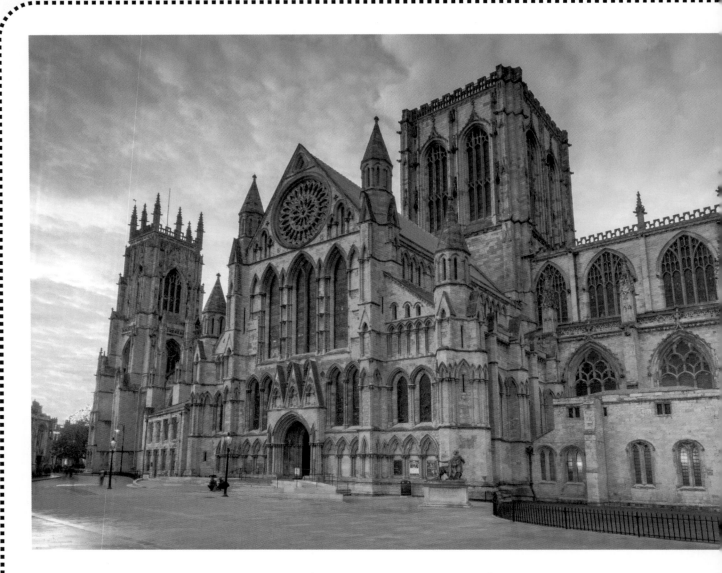

York Minister, York

Counties

There are 48 counties in England;
Greater London, West Midlands, Greater Manchester, West Yorkshire, Kent, Hampshire, Essex, Lancashire, Merseyside, South Yorkshire, Devon, Surrey, Hertfordshire, North Yorkshire, Nottinghamshire, Tyne and Wear, Staffordshire. Lincolnshire, Cheshire, Leicestershire, Derbyshire, Somerset, Gloucestershire, Berkshire, Norfolk, Durham, West Sussex, Cambridgeshire, East Sussex, Buckinghamshire, Dorset, Suffolk, Northamptonshire, Wiltshire, Oxfordshire, Bedfordshire, East Riding of Yorkshire, Worcestershire, Warwickshire, Cornwall, Cumbria, Shropshire, Bristol, Northumberland, Herefordshire, Isle of Wight, Rutland and City of London.

English schoolgirl

Population

England has population of **55.9 million people** making it the most populated country in the United Kingdom.

England has a relatively high population density, with an average of around 430 people per square kilometre. The population of England is diverse and dynamic, with a mix of urban and rural areas, a range of cultural influences, and a long history of immigration and settlement.

Street in London

Size

England is **130,279 square kilometres** making it the largest country in the United Kingdom by area.

Despite its small size, England has a diverse landscape that includes rolling hills, rugged coastlines, and verdant countryside. England is home to several major cities, including London, Manchester, Birmingham, Liverpool, and Newcastle.

Languages

The national language of England is English. The English language originated in England and is now spoken by hundreds of millions of people across the world.

Cornish is a regional language of England.

Here are a few English phrases and sayings
- **It's raining cats and dogs -** It is raining heavily
- **Let the cat out of the bag -** Reveal a secret
- **Break a leg -** Good luck

Tower Bridge, London

Attractions

There are lots of interesting places to see in England.

Some beautiful places to visit in England are

- **Buckingham Palace**
- **Tower of London**
- **The Shard**
- **Tower Bridge**
- **Hampton Court Palace**
- **The Cotswolds**

Arundel Castle, England

History of England

People have lived in England for a very long time. It is believed that humans have inhabited England from as much as 800,000 years ago.

Continuous human habitation in England dates back to around 13,000 years ago when the Last Glacial Period ended.

In AD 43 the Roman conquest of Britain began and the Romans maintained control of their province of Britannia until the early 5th century.

Customs in England

England has many fascinating customs and traditions.

- Pub culture is an integral part of British culture. A pub is a place where people gather together for drinks.
- Afternoon Tea is common in England. In an Afternoon tea, people meet together for some cakes, sandwiches and tea.
- Every Christmas Day, the monarch of the country delivers a national televised speech.

Glastonbury Festival

Music of England

There are many different music genres in England such as **beat music, psychedelic music, progressive rock/pop, heavy metal, grime and new wave.**

Some notable English musicians include
- **Ed Sheeran**
- **Sam Smith**
- **One Direction**
- **Stormzy**
- **Sade**
- **The Beatles**

Chicken Tikka Masala

Food of England

Traditional English cuisine is known for its hearty, simple, and comforting dishes.

The national dish of England is **Chicken tikka masala,** a delicious Indian Curry which is often served with rice or bread.

Food of England

English cuisine has a long history and is influenced by a variety of factors, including the country's geography, climate, and cultural heritage.

Some popular dishes in England include

- **Bangers and mash: This is a simple and hearty dish made with sausages and mashed potatoes.**
- **Full English breakfast: This is a hearty breakfast meal that typically includes eggs, bacon, sausages, grilled tomatoes, mushrooms, black pudding, and toast.**

Bradford City Hall, England

Weather in England

England has a temperate maritime climate. Weather remains mild throughout the year and rainfall is common.

The coldest months fall between **December to February.**

Two sheep in Shropshire

Animals of England

There are many wonderful animals in England.

Here are some animals that live in England

- **Squirrels**
- **Frogs**
- **Foxes**
- **Rodents**
- **Hares**

Brighton Beach, England

Beaches

There are many beautiful beaches in England which is one of the reasons why so many people visit this beautiful country every year.

Here are some of England's beaches

- **Southend Beach**
- **Brighton Beach**
- **Bournemouth Beach**
- **Hastings Beach**
- **Blackpool Beach**

England football fan

Sports of England

Sports play an integral part in English culture. The most popular sport is **Football.**

Here are some of famous sportspeople from England

- **Jonathan Edwards - Athletics**
- **Andy Murray - Tennis**
- **Harry Kane - Football**
- **Wayne Rooney - Football**
- **David Beckham - Football**
- **Alan Shearer - Football**

Famous

Many successful people hail from England.

Here are some notable English figures

- **Winston Churchill – Former Prime Minister**
- **Diana, Princess of Wales – Princess**
- **William Shakespeare – Writer**
- **Isaac Newton – Physicist**
- **John Lennon – Musician**
- **Queen Elizabeth II - Monarch**

Stonehenge, England

Something Extra...

As a little something extra, we are going to share some lesser known facts about England

- England fought the shortest war in history
- England is the birthplace of many famous scientists such as Isaac Newton and Charles Darwin
- The World Wide Web was invented in England.

Westminster Abbey, London

Words From the Author

We hope that you enjoyed learning about the wonderful country of England.

England is a country rich in culture and beauty, with lots of wonderful places to visit and people to meet.

We hope you continue to learn more about this wonderful nation. If you enjoyed this book, consider leaving a review!

With Love